The Abandoned Country

Books by Thomas Rabbitt

Exile
The Booth Interstate
The Abandoned Country

The Abandoned Country

poems by
Thomas Rabbitt

Carnegie Mellon University Press
Pittsburgh 1988

Acknowledgments

Some of the poems included here, some in different versions or with different titles, have appeared in other publications: "Researching Lost Time" in *Antaeus*; "Asylum," "The Saint and Her Betrayer," "Timber Sales," "Christmas Gifts," "September 1, 1983," "Tortoise" and "Losses" in *The Black Warrior Review*; "My Father's Watch" in *Ploughshares*; "The Dogs of War" in *Poetry*; "A Prospect of Diamonds Out Back," "The Cemetery at Blanco," "Drunk Tank," "The Cannibal Murders on Brick Kiln Road" and "The Line" in *The Poetry Miscellany*; "Dust Bowl Preacher" in *Shenandoah*; "The Chinese Satyricon" in *The University of Windsor Review*.

"Dust Bowl Preacher" published as "Sirocco" and "Psalm" in *Shenandoah*, copyright 1977 by Washington and Lee University, reprinted from *Shenandoah:* The Washington and Lee University Review with permission of the editor.

The publication of this book is supported by grants from the National Endowment for the Arts in Washington, D.C., a Federal agency, and by the Pennsylvania Council on the Arts.

Carnegie Mellon University Press books are distributed by Harper and Row, Publishers.

Contents

for Beatrice DeAvilla

I sent myself out forever on roads.
I'll never be home except here, dirt poor
in abandoned country. My enemy, wind,
helps me hack each morning again at the rock.

—Richard Hugo

Tortoise

I guess today's another day among the days
When nothing ever happens well,
Another afternoon lost drinking, rocker
Jammed against the front porch wall.
Spring. And it has just stopped raining. Two boys
Come loping up the muddy road.
The boys decide to stop, unload their load,
A turtle on the porch for me to praise,
Which I do, I do, box turtle, which they say
They found abandoned and alone
And nearly dead beside the road
And will I let them put it in my pond.
I will. I do. And when, just like a stone,
It sinks and does not rise again, I say,
Don't worry, turtles always sink this way.
The boys spend hours watching and I sit back
To drink my beer. The ducks raise hell. The sun
Setting lights up the water while the boys
Gaze out over the pond. They shake their heads
And take this as their loss. Yes, I can lie.
Yes, I will tell them what I do not know.

The Cemetery at Blanco

He tends his graves. I walk with his wife
To a dim brown corner of the graveyard where
We wonder why the nineteenth century Hungarians
Decorated their dead with scallop shells.
Watch out, he yells, *for rattlers*. Does he mean me?
I can tell her nearly nothing, what I can guess
From the stones, what she can see: twin infant girls
And then their mother, dead in days; the second wife,
Her husband's sons; her and him; the long slow
Dying out of generations. No rattlesnakes.
No plagues or Texas cattle wars. Just scallop shells.

The wife has her ideas, the husband his
Of what we've come to find among these dead.
Around us Blanco County's dull gold hills roll off
Into fictions. He drags a garden hose
Like a green snake across the parched boneyard.
A sapling. His daddy's grave. His wife. And me.
These improbabilities cannot connect.
The center of the universe has frightened me.
The air is full of soft Comanche cries, scrub oak,
The view toward town, a family whose funerals I missed.
Here lies your wife and son. This grave is yours.

Here, where all the world is held in place
On stone by dates, the dead are saying, *Comfort*.
The highway is silent. In the hills, cattle ease
From dusty meal to meal. Beneath the mesquite
A thousand years wait with the rattlesnakes—
Out there, or here, watching my friends and me.
There are a few flowers, a redtail hawk, some shrubs.
The graveyard slopes—I shouldn't tell—like a bed,

From pillow to foot, downhill, gentle, orderly,
Across the highway and into the dried up river bed.

He is done with his daddy as he is.
She and I watch him coil the hose too carefully.
Drought makes the matter-of-fact seem less so.
I understand. The dead have broken through their shells
And are crying, *Water! Water!* But he moves on
To his pickup. Then his wife moves with him.
I am standing in the center of distance. Of dust.
The wampum covered graves are dusty, like the hills,
The cattle, the highway, the town and the river,
White with the dust the living stir as they leave.
This is the easy end where what I want to say is:
Leave me. Take yourselves and your hose away,
Your oaks and your hills into kinder weather.
I understand and I am not afraid. Leave me.

The Dogs of War

1. *Fishing at Dawn*

You lift the last bass gasping from the lake
And on the other shore, hemmed in by a circle
Of dark pines, the neighbors rise to applaud.
What are they doing out so early?
I think they have been watching for ships.
The dog beside you, beside himself, dances over
His reflection on the wet bank and the fish stops
Hung midair. You seem to ponder his loss:
The colder principality where he saw and heard
Our blood thrumming and our eyes bearing light
Against him. His descent to the dog takes no time
At all. If we waited, we could will fish
Out of trees, trees from fish, lovers from the lake.

Dedication brings the bass to the dog.
Dedication saves them. If you could, some days
You'd throw us all back in. The trees, the neighbors,
The yapping dog. But here, by the lake, a wave
Of new love strikes me while the neighbors
Are changing the guard. There are no fish left.
No dogs. No lovers. The neighbors have gone back
To their beds. If we stop now, we're saved.
The bass sees mercy. The dog knows that you reach
For a larger hook. Only I know better.
You fish with minnows, even though,
When hooked through the eyes, they're easy to lose.

You fish the same spot, catch the one fish.
Always the same neighbors, the same looks.
Always the dog gone crazy for the struggling fish.
Why do I stay here to watch? The trees stay.

The neighbors, like lifeguards, whistle and hoot
From the other bank and new love strikes
Through the broken water. It is always the same.
Dedication dies hard or never dies.
The group of us climbs the hill to the new house.
We admire the wild magnolia fanning their huge
Papery leaves around us. The flowers reflect light
And smell like lemons. I can hear you think:
Tomorrow, at last, we can all go hungry.
In front of us the sun rises naked and fat
Teasing a savage fire out of your eyes.

2. *The Fire around Us*

On the hill behind the house trees rise and rise,
Their tops building cathedrals over the fire.
A near world burns. The entire horizontal fills
With small animals, fox and rabbit and coon,
Whose hearts move faster than their slow legs.
See how the cottonmouth slides free of the fire.
They come in all directions out, burning like sin,
Like the souls in Purgatory who call for our prayers.
Deer and squirrels and quail, the birds walking
Aflame, the dark wild eyes like rubies in the fire.
The animals have no choice. They flee well.
You open the kitchen door. I stand with the hose
Ready in the garden. The fires fall downhill.

You tell them, we die more than myth can bear today.
We open our rooms to them, our clean beds,
We open ourselves because we know
There's no way to keep them from us. No way.
I run in all directions with the hose. I joke,
Say I'm pissing into the wind. They feel better.
And you laugh. The soot thickening your eyes is like
Your dark preparations for a party. We'll leave soon.
It's our charity that evicts us, that and your rare
Touch burns everyone to the bone. At these moments
Your eyes are most beautiful and the house inviting.

3. *On the Road to a Party*

Some evenings even the flowers look like disaster:
Their heads glow like lightbulbs ready to burst
When dropped. Their colors, body fluids, red
And yellow, break through skin calling,
We are too beautiful for you. Don't look.
By the roadside, lovers pull through song,
Push and pull in the breaking grass and cars
Passing careen to avoid them. Odd that we choose
To love in spots where dogs have died, where
We roll like mongrels in the thick scent of loss.

Day lilies burn out in Alabama sideyards.
Hydrangeas hold the round faces of blue babies
Against the sun, pale, delicate and too many.
All today's heroes could be born dead.
You, with your ear to the ground, you hear things
Rumbling toward us. First a train driving
Itself to death. Then a heart pounding
Out of the nearest house. Last, armies
Of the Old South which never stops marching through.
Calla lilies and the first Red Cross,
Cotton bolls and semen strung on bushes,
Honeysuckle lifting our bones into the wind.

Someone could kill you for not existing, kill you
For lifting your face to each car that slows
And honks as it passes. Mad and lonely, the new moon
Will still go over. Black faces will glint at us
Out of houses and near trees. Deadly, alien
Mimosas, the willows old enough to shade graves.
The water covers the lakes. The faces are young

15

And they know: there is no you here.
The water lilies resign. They all lost touch.
Disaster seems correct. Don't look.
Tonight we are still too beautiful for you.

4. Driving Home at Night

On the last drive home, drunk, from a party
You say, seasons startle children and young dogs
Who never have seen snow. Or, sorrow fits the ruts
To the lake. Maybe the lives of saints.
The death of a younger son. Perhaps. If it matters.
I hear the dogs chasing us from this road to the next.
What will we do, ever do, when they catch us?
You say we can swallow the truck. Or save bullets,
One for the other. Now you tell me that you're pregnant.
The child wants us to drive headlong into the lake
Where the thick weeds rise and wave over pearls.
I don't think it is a good idea. Remember their eyes?

The trees recall failure. I recall old phone numbers
And fallen kings. If I die, you have photographs
To carry on. Look. The highway needs nothing
To make us glad. The headlights are fiddling
In the darkness just beyond our lungs. The radio cries.
And you say that I'll smile at anything at night.
I could press your body hard against each tree
And none of them would cry like the old stories
Of girls imprisoned in trees. So I've buried
The mortgage where you want the flower garden.
The neighbors say the grass still looks like failure.
It's adaptation keeps the pines from fire.

I stay alive to watch the peacocks spread their eyes.
Don't drag me from the trees. Tonight I feel as good
As furniture, ripe and usable as chairs.
Today I have watched you break apart like every woman
I have ever known, our losses like the weeds

Our best friends say should never be allowed to grow.
What do they know? Their parties bury us in bones.
Dogs or friends dig us up again. Love is natural.
If you want, I'll be a garden, color eating through
The green—red and yellow marigolds, success.

At night, at ninety miles an hour, let's press against
The first black walnut or live oak. We can rise
Out of ourselves, over and over, green on brown,
Singing like a pair of old nuns at High Mass.
You say I smile at anything. Just beyond your lungs.
The headlights weave through trees, the tires spin
Silly on the shoulder. The radio still goes.
The pines and kudzu go. The curves fill with futures.
Let's say we're very old now and we're driving home.
From the hospital or the church. Let's say we've buried
One another. The same stray dogs want to chase us.
Let's say they've wasted their lives for food.

When I steer at them, the trees give like real people.
We've never been so much in love. We've never tried.

Staying on Alone

I am pretending to be old, that you
Aren't dead. Today your family has come
To take your clothes and books back home.
I ask them leave me you. They say
It is warm in Paris, it is cold, it snows,
Oui, non. They smile like bankers.
It is warm. They count your shoes.

Tell me the world is not ourselves.
It is a small garden where potatoes grow.
Or tell me it is like the race course
In the woods. Tell me.
I can believe that we are both.

Here in the woods of Boulogne faces crop
Out of trees. For one, yours. You are grey,
What you must look like now,
Skin like old food, dead and left
Underground where it will keep.

They have taken down your paintings,
Left my walls, left me old bright spaces
Like a chessboard. Time tells, time plays.
When I go out I see in the trees of Boulogne
My lifetime. I see your faces
Smiling out of the bark. The touch is grey.
I feel dead, that all I am is waiting.

The Buzzard on the Barnyard Gate

i.

The palomino mare, afterbirth tangled
In her tail, sways like a drunken nanny
Over the corpse of her foal. This one was money
In the bank. The buzzard snakes her naked head
And waits. You never know, you never know,
So you eat it as it lies, in rain or snow
Or under the blazon of a bright late April sky.
I eat, you eat, the feathered shadow feasts.
Money in the bank, crickets drowning in the water tank,
The cats and dogs and chickens run from death.
The nanny takes her aching belly to the riverbank.
I think she suffers from a loss of faith.

ii.

I catch the mare and hide her in a stall.
It's not your fault, I say, it's not your fault at all.
The buzzard, gone aloft, is back to say I lie.
She'll wait, the black-gold substitute for song.
Chained to the tractor, the dead filly slits
A furrow from the barnyard to the swamp.
Should I call this a plowing in of profits?
What I do when I dump to rot my loss
Under the budding sycamore and oak?
Far from the fencerows lies the heart, too far
For the buzzard to smell or see, so far
I have trouble finding the right way back.

Dust Bowl Preacher

Beaver, Oklahoma, 1934

1. *Sirocco*

What can be and what I know I heard from a man
On his knees in the dust, praying
Into the fistfuls of dust until he had saved it all.
Rabies can come from dust.
Already you fear water, your cracked throat, the noise
Of flies drumming at the screen door.

It might rain.
Everything could be mud, more salvations
Than the world can use. Each wind carries your farm
To the door, carries night, the howling of sick fox
In the woods. The mad black racer is a slithering noose
Hissing under your henhouse. The snake has always been
Sliding through history.
He sucks eggs and drives the rooster crazy.

He remembers
Lifting into the wind, carrying the worst death,
The death above death. He moves into the kitchen and out,
Away from the barnyard, the farm, away from our town
And our drought, away from ourselves and the dust.
He moves into the city. He breathes into the houses,
The fast streets, the many people who cannot bear death.
Remember? The dog, the fox, the curled black snake,
All poultry and houses and streets
Pick themselves up in the wind. Flight is the last,
The best communion. He goes with them. He comforts them.
He knows words of creation.

The city marches away. The mayor clutches his throat,
And houses are afraid of the noise.

21

The flies go drowsy, marching afoot.
We are the fiddles of plague, they say, stopping
To scrape at their legs. All things line up behind them.
The taut rope they tread is the safest way. He follows,
Wishing them a dry wind, a difficult death, sainthood.

2. *Psalm*

Our women pretend that they are apple trees and ask
Their men to carve them into boxes for the keeping
Of their children's work.
Our men have doffed their brainpans and go begging.
But, Lord, it is not terrible.
But for you, it could be worse.
There might be only luck and those of us
Who cleaned our skulls smoother than the barber's basin.
You have promised to ignore the idiot who sings and rocks
Against his crib and knows as well as you
That six or seven sets of milk teeth are his.

We are swimming toward you, Lord, through the jellied seas
Of prophets. There is a taste of burnt tongues
And your people harvest what you say.
It is a six-day landscape, our parade, and a missing truth
Is easy since it waits. We do not mind, we never say
We mind. We only travel. It is your country, Lord,
And we will eat whatever organ meats you think
Will exercise our teeth. We will gnaw then
On the seven smiling dolours of the Virgin.
These are extra thistles larding the heart of our messiah.

The mountains burn. She thanks us for that spoon
The martyr carved from broken fibula
While, pointing in, she empties out another.

The Line

If you don't own half of Kansas
You need to live by the sea.
Otherwise, day and night are surprises,
Hostage to one or another tree.

Horses are dropping off the edge of the world
Into gullies Prince Valiant said he feared.
The Sierra Club has made me ashamed of my farm.
The horses, when they fall, turn their heads
On long lovely necks and, through the sad drop,
Gaze back at my guilt. What eyes they have!
This catastrophe was always my fault.
I would like to blame the weather, the years
Of wind and rain washing my fields to sea.
I would call it sandy clay or call it gestalt.
One month, one morning, a new horizon
Yawns closer till the fence rows collapse
And the curious dumb beasts follow the wires
Over the edge of the earth. I can see ships,
Dragon-ships, plodding across the bottom of the sky.
Once upon a time a circle of dark pines.
Once a difference between here and gone.
A sorrel mare is tumbling off today's flat earth
And she has to know that her fall is too long,
That though she will land, that I will come for her,
As of course I have, she will have already died.
My gun is as useless as music and the line
I never trusted surrounds us overhead.

Asylum

1. *Christmas Day*

His wife was unfaithful for money, his daughter
Went blind, her eyes like blue lace and cold
In his mother's house where it was Christmas.
The men in the other beds want him, want to pump
At his wrists, to suck the poisons of his blood.
An ecstasy of razors, their lunacy eats out his eyes.

Symptoms of the past, lives of women he still eyes,
Are like bones found in backyards. His daughter
Is a disease to stumble on. The days grow cold.
But the sun over his bed, still as bright as Christmas,
Like Mother's tree, his needles, the stomach pump.
He thinks deep down he is happy drowning in blood.

It is safe under bandages where the blood
Has dried in spots to look back at him like eyes.
They are the pale eyes of his daughter,
Raveling and nearly gone. She thinks it very cold
In her grandmother's house, strange this Christmas.
Her blind screams work on his gut like another pump.

Doctor, he has visions of a woman turned to a pump
Where you put in coins and babies or blood
Come out. He wants to insert his eyes.
Or can I, he asked, leave them to my daughter?
Doctor, he says to tell you the ward is cold,
That he can't last the twelve days to Little Christmas.

She was gone a week and then came back on Christmas
Just to see the baby. He called her the pump
House whore, in a whore's Christmas dress, blood
Red, and with a painted whore's fat green eyes.

25

He said, go kiss your daughter,
And the girl said, no, your hands are cold.

The ward light is always on. The sheets are cold.
He can hear the attendants talking about Christmas,
Hear them at night, in the grey halls, over the pump
Pump of his heart moving the unwanted blood
To any escape. Hands. Mouth. Eyes.
Yes, he said, just give me money for my daughter.

He woke and told them that he wanted to pump blood
Out of himself and into his daughter's cold eyes.
Like Jesus, he could give her a vision for Christmas.

2. *New Year's Eve*

Your mother sits at home and sees in runs your touch
Grow red. She remembers: Mary Griffin's son went mad,
Shot her, killed himself. Now Mary's crippled on one side.
Boy, you can never come here again. One last kiss
And she disowns you. You might kill them all in the night.
New Year's Eve. Her children have driven her to drink.

A thousand miles away big brother swills a drink,
Beer and bourbon and just the right touch
Of wives, colleagues and contempt to drive him mad.
He tries to take refuge, but there is no safe side,
In or out. Flesh runs off faces like a friend's kiss
To leave skulls, the future and a quick goodnight.

In her country house your sister prepares for a night
On the town. Yesterday, when you asked for a drink
Of water, the attendants would not let you touch.
So now, she thinks, this is what it means to go mad,
To marry well, to get locked up, each on one side
Of safety, where it is correct never again to kiss.

Your daughter hears the light click, waits for the kiss.
She rears her blank face to your wife's good night,
Feels the wet, smells the Avon and the sour drink.
Her mother's hair is long and dry to the touch.
Your daughter pulls it till she knows her mother's mad.
If she gets slapped she can cry and turn on her side.

Like two tethered boats pitching from side to side
Your wife and her current lover bump and kiss
The expensive hours away by midnight.
Later she makes him take her out for a drink

27

In a bar where others will come for the next touch.
She knows it was this and a smile that drove you mad.

In the ward at midnight lights flash and the mad-
Men begin to cheer. From the other side
Of the locked door the cheers are howls, a kiss
From the past meant to last a lifetime or a night.
Boy, do you remember? Someone tried to bring you a drink
Of water and the attendant would not let you touch.

Later in the same night you feel a touch
Quivering against your side, then a wet kiss.
You give the mad queer a mouthful of blood to drink.

3. *Epiphany*

No, Doctor, I've experimented. It's hard to die.
You can't just think about it, lie back and close
Your eyes and wonder which death needs the least help.
Not death, but dying is what's hard. Death's a smile,
Looks like what you want, pretty, handsome, clean
As a bone. Each death fits a woman or a man.

One of them came last night in the shape of a man.
He touched me. He said, I hear you want to die.
The men in the ward are always too close,
Always there with hands and lips too ready to help.
Old. And they've got no teeth when they smile
And there's one who keeps saying, my boy, I'm clean.

You don't think I know how fucking old and clean
He is, so washed out he might really be a woman?
Is this what you do before you let us die,
Scrub away our bodies and our brains so when you close
The coffin there's nothing but picked bones to help
The worms with? Nothing but my skull's lovely smile?

Dying's easy. The death's head's not a smile.
It's a grin. The old man ain't so clean
Where it counts. So he's really not a man,
But your grandmother you've brought here to die.
I like grandmothers. I like the way they close
Their mouths inside the shout for help.

There's a nurse like a sail who wants to bring me help.
She comes in in the mornings to swab my wrists. I smile
When she blows in, dressed like a bandage, as clean
As a sail. I shout, it's time! Time to man

The lifeboats! Abandon ship or die!
Sink or swim, let go, the hurricane's too close.

Doctor, when you go under, do all your women close
In like the three gifts? Gold won't help,
Not incense or oils. What I want—my wife to smile
At me for a change, my daughter to see, my arms clean
Of the tracks—I want. *Ecce homo*. Behold the man,
A bad joke when you're always about to die.

Your asylum has a wicked smile chock full of help
And bad teeth. They say, clean yourself up, man.
It's close. They want to say something before you die.

My Father's Watch

From Boston south he talks of citrus fruit
And extra children who pop like extra toes.
A good man cuts them off or he makes room.
His girlfriend looks like she will never laugh.
There is an old man who lived in shoes,
Refinished basements, plastered catacombs
Where the cold walls felt like a dead son's face.
Sons are lemons: yellow, sour, small and tough.
Atlantic City. We stop to play roulette.
Chamber to chamber our winnings grow.
Next day, the pike Russia, the pavement slick,
He tells her: in the basement room my son
And I held pistols to our heads and played
For laughs. His world outside of time is charmed.
In Delaware no child has ever died.
We stop in Baltimore to buy the watch.
He knows which street. From alley to alley,
Block to block, he hears it tick. The harbor rolls.
When wound my father's watch goes *click*.
The sound the bottom makes before it drops
And the Oldsmobile skids into Florida.
British frigates are bombarding Fort McHenry.
His luggage, his bankbook, his girlfriend and I
Spill into the sunshine. Now he is retired.
His yellow watch carries him, every nervous tick
Counting the walls of each new empty room.

Christmas Gifts

So, friend, wish for this: an angel swoops
Through the parlor curtains and gives your wife
The right name for all things. I do mean all.
Later, in bed, she says it's called omniscience.
Words being what they are, words lead one
To another. Your wife cannot be brief.
You'll never get a second question in.

The rain has stopped. Like a tease, ground fog lifts
Through the yard light. Asleep in her bright gift
Your wife mumbles a running sound. Like water,
Like waves drawing smooth pebbles back
Into the full sea, she is all words.
Fog drips from the bronzed hydrangeas.
The winter manages to seep in.

Breakfast. The ordeal of champions. Listen:
The new stallion is breaking down the barn.
Your wife in pink curlers and purple scarf
Is turning the new kitchen to stone.
It's rock soup, the con-man's finest tale,
Her light touch, green thumb and now, like a laugh,
Poised on her lips, new worlds according to fact.

Today could ruin love. Listen: the phone rings.
Your mother wins the Irish Derby. A letter comes.
Your first, most silken girlfriend's back in town.
Like Christmas a shiny angel sidles up to everyone
With beauty, youth, power and renown. Sacks full.
Your marriage wishes more: a gift of tongues,
One prophecy, one child who didn't have to drown.

At midnight the cattle are supposed to talk.
Two thousand years of servile plaster scenes.

A hard rain makes the barn roof ring,
Makes you wonder if you'll ever live to hear
What the livestock have to say. Tin and rain,
Tin and rain, a wife, dry hay, the pain itself
Speaking itself over and over and over again.

The Chinese Satyricon
North Beach, October, 1969

1. *A Garden off Green Street*

At twilight a young man cracks his garden gate, peers
Into the street and asks you in. His name is Dan.
His smile moves across the tall silvery fence bounding
His garden and lights on the carelessly broken head
Of an aster. It's how we tell the autumn from the dead,
He says, and I'm older than I look, he says, bending
To snap the stem. He asks you again to come in
And when you do his smile breaks down into tears.
His sad voice echoes off the neighbors' walls.
They watch from their kitchens, he says, they watch
And hope to catch me and you in some obscenity.
Look. In their concrete basin the gold fish understand.
The nasturtiums and the mums want to understand.
We're all older than we look, but there's still
Plenty of time. His hand moves to the gate latch.
It was good having you, Dan says. We've all
Enjoyed having you. He settles, slowly, into a wicker chair.
If you come again, he says, I shall probably be here.

2. *Across the Back Fence*

The smell from the chicken processing plant
Wasn't so bad today. Today it was the poultry cries
Rising above the traffic and all those prayers sifting
Across the back fence and into the Back Fence Bar.
The bartender says that some days he just can't bear
To hear them chickens screech, the sound of it lifting
Over the neighborhood. Each time a chicken dies
Some drunk asks, What's that? The bartender just can't
Bear to say. And then, when the women come in

34

After work, their arms still slick to the elbows
With all that digging at guts and blood,
Then he wants to ask them why they do it.
That kind of work just can't be worth it.
But the ladies don't mind much. Everyone's had to bleed
So many chickens, read so many piled high rows
Of guts, that it don't much matter, even to women.
But to hear them and smell them both is never good
For business, except for the bars in the neighborhood.

3. The Year of the Rooster Dance

At the Back Fence old men wait outside the pay toilet
For you to exit. You suspect they want one or the other,
But as they push past, one mentions that
It costs near as much to piss it out as put it down.
What you want to say is, Well, you're on your own,
Old man, a big boy now. He tips his hat.
In one corner of the bar a crowd begins to gather
Around the pet rooster from the chicken processing plant.
A young man, yes, it is Dan, moves to the flashing jukebox
And makes it play The Tennessee Waltz.
The rooster rears back, flaps his wings and crows.
The crowd opens and closes like a dying heart
And the rooster claws at the sawdust. His feet start
With the music. He makes circles as if he knows
This is what pleases you about life the most.
The old man comes from the restroom. I'm the fox,
He says, joining the dance. Still, the rooster never stops
His circling until the man clutches his throat and drops.

4. The Bridge

Dan hates this city and has to love his garden
On account, he says, of the dove under the little bridge
Like a new world troll and the tiny people he can guess
Are going past the railings on their hands and knees
So you can't see them. You wonder what he knows
And you will never, that the blue sky and black bridge press
Together like a bruise, that each edge
Spanning goes nowhere and that he *can* see them,
The people who are crawling across, caught up there
Between newscasts. It's late evening, but there's light
Enough for them to see each other pass. A distant town
Glows like a snail's track in the dark.
Their torn hands, knuckles bleeding, grub along, stark
In the moonlight they inch across. If love looks down
It sees Dan looking up, things grown huge, his eyes bright
With progress, what he once called the perpetual care
Of his garden's corpse. Frustration, he says, feeds
This life. Dig it up or bury it, the garden still seeds.

5. Calliope

From the bed you can see across the moonlit alley
Into the Chinaman's house where he, in his parlor, sits
Dying. His women rise around him like heathen screams
Whose patience must hold you quiet. Dan, guilty, thrills
Like a sick tooth, and you claw at the only process that fills
The blacked-out windows. Theirs is the sound of dreams.
You roll over yourselves for the view, to see if it all fits:
The mourning, the old moon's lambence silvering the alley,
The tintype music of the calliope playing in the bar

On the next block. Dan gets up to make coffee.
The Chinese women subside. The calliope is louder.
From the kitchen Dan wonders whether the moon moving
Will fill your window and show you for what you are, proving
You have no shame, naked at his death, and prouder.
It's like a daguerreotype, silver and black, the calliope,
The moonlight and the man, blurred, caught from afar
Through the glass. It's the old invention that erases
With light your thrumming blood, your fingerprints and faces.

The Pet Shop Arsonist

The expensive puppies sleep with their paws
Through the bars of their cages. They should know
What makes cages. Collies, poodles or chows,
They dream what they will be and wait, tier
On tier, shitty puppies sleeping in cages.
There is such little light. The opposite wall
Is gold guppies and bubbles and blue light
Which doesn't count, being such little light.
The fish sleep too, fanning darkness to stay afloat.
Black mollies have to be bored with their lives.
The prospect of plumage. The prospect! Look
Above the pet goods, in open aviaries,
The rarest birds sit, green models for coins.
Plants, potted and plastic, a display case
Of snakes, white mice, gerbils, siamese cats,
And a chattering squirrel monkey awake
In his room in the window, watching for thieves.

The power dies. The bubbling in the tanks
Is heat, then the betas slow-motion beating
Lifts them to the surface through the duck weed.
When the fish tanks burst, water's not enough.
So now the fire is eating cats and dogs
Asleep in their glowing cages and dreaming
Of sleep. The light is turning to a pink dawn.
The cockatoos will never be more gorgeous
Than right now, aflame, flying for the ceiling.
The snakes crawling over and over again
Out of their crackling skins can get nowhere.
The shop has filled itself with perfect air.
The monkey is tapping the window glass.
Being himself, the monkey wants to look

Almost human. The flames fill his background.
He turns to tell the others what he sees.

For Those Who Will Live Forever

The law said Dale Booth died of falling.
Some nights Dell Booth sits at home and drinks.
His wife talks on. Dell sits and stares
Through the thin pane of his picture window
Down through the burned pines to the highway.
He thinks that everyone is moving away.
The glass shakes. Dale Booth died at two,
Aged two, at two in the morning, of falling
When Dell, falling, could not bear the screaming
And pulled the blocks from beneath his son's end
Of their mobile home. Some nights, late, Dell thinks
He hears a child calling from the tall goldenrod
Near the roadway. *Sorry. Sorry.* But it is only
A possum or dog some car has killed.

Drunk Tank

1.

Somewhere—in a hive of light and shadow—
A drunk is calling, *Innocent! Innocent!*
And a pope calls back, *Si* and *Ciao.*
The first drunk sobs. The second laughs too loud.
The county jail is crammed with intellect.
Call it gratitude, release, the dim
Invention of their lives: lights, steel, the bars.
There are too many men in the same small cell.

2.

No heat. The smell of urine. Three low watt lights.
Three shadows of a suicide dance from floor
To ceiling and free, through the bars
Out into the corridor.
For as long as it takes to die
The shadows move toward unity and then some.
The hanged boy sways the architecture's lie.

Who'd have thought the air was so unstill?
That dance could be as temperate as ice?
His eyes bulge with his last surprise.
One drunk wakes up and yells, *I'm dead!*
This ain't no dream, my God, I'm dead. Overhead
The dead boy floats, coming and going
With a dead boy's scorn for cells.

3.

The guards were cautious, sure it was a hoax.
Now a captain tapes the corpse-lines to the wall.
The artist in him, with just one twist,

Captures the odd angle of the dead boy's neck.
Adhesive reaches to the ceiling and across,
To the grid over the light. The line is taut.
Two more shadows traced and the corpse falls.
Softer than his expectations he lies heaped
Like soggy cardboard on the concrete floor.

4.

The suicide is taken down, covered up, carried
To the sidewalk, dumped. I think of Paris
Or Loudon, those wonderful years
When the gutters filled with plague
And the Sun-King trained his bees
To gather blood.

5.

Interrogation
When we drunks rehearse just what it was we saw.
Everyone was asleep and dreaming
Of an inner room in a painter's studio.
We looked out from canvas onto canvas,
Painting ourselves or being painted
Like those clever matinee cartoons growing
From the artist's drawn and drawing hand.

Perspective seems to be a problem for us,
Marooned as we are by blood and excrement
On the beige tiles that interrupt the bars.
Our signatures are as delicate as the bees
Who gather our faces into hexagrams,

Whose eyes have it, staring like mementos
From the best earth tones of all.

6.

The drunk tank is booked one voice at a time.
The best drunks last to carry on like Carmelites
A decreasing dialogue of heads.

Madame Sergeant, why do you write so fast?
Is music so corrupting to your soul? Look.
The Reign of Terror lives, has always lived
Around us. Look. Whole county jails can lose
Their heads so fast it saints them. Listen.
Down the hall a drunk whore's singing *Summertime*
Though it is winter and all your bees do sleep.

A Prospect of Diamonds Out Back

A small trek from house to barn occupies
My morning like a cardiac arrest.
I'd avoid this; I can't. So I enjoy
As the onanist enjoys his daily death.
My farm is a salesman's dream,
Monkey paw or wild ass's skin, grown
But for trash a measure smaller each time
It's sold, each day it suffers rain.
I know that I must drink too much.
Erosion satisfies me, slowly, from within.

Would you wonder that a barn might loom
At fifty feet? Hog briar and cracked shale loom.
The night's dropped rain can loom.
The red clay, slick as a lover's tongue,
And the barn, a symphony in rust, these loom.
Everything I own reminds me that it must
Be fed or else will die on my hands.
In one pocket one hand looms
To accomplish nothing. One hand totes a pail,
One hand feels the air against my face,
One hand pulls my hair. All hands fail.

I buy this farm in order to be saved.
Payments haven't worked that way.
Horses, goats, dogs, chickens, the debits
Of a grossly other life. Subtract one day
After another from that life, till one knows why
This land is never held, is never sold,
Is simply left like a child's tooth
To be redeemed from the wrinkled sheets
And sweat by a dream of any day's success.
Each night it rains. Clay and sand wash off

The rough edges of a predecessor's trash.
Each dawn lights the light of their success.

And so I pass it. On the way from house
To barn. And though I see it shine
I know it can be nothing more than glass,
A bright lozenge turned up from a mine
Of all the scattered, mortgaged trash
Onanists have used to seed the land.
Take pride. Take pleasure. Please. Stay undeceived.
The livestock love you. Yes, the horses do.
The rising sun nibbles daylight from your hand.

On the path back to the house the lozenge
Eats at your eyes. It was never glass.
I think you too should settle for the truth:
For the dark blue stone cut like clear cobalt,
For the gold cord disguised as baling twine.
You will sit like me, digging with a Cree axhead
At a half-buried square of whitest ivory.
All failure is remote. You will be glad,
Like me, to stay here, carefully, forever.
You will give up prospects, your job, your wife.
Half-buried, important ivory, color, shape,
This bathroom tile from other people's lives.
We will have to help each other, we must decide.

Timber Sales

The trees are in their autumn beauty, dry
Although it's winter, nearly spring, and fire
Rises from my neighbor's hills like plague.
All night wild birds and tiny insects sing:
This is no war to bring a lover to.
Yellow skidders, like life from the moon, falling
All night through space, are landed now; steel teeth
Are eating trees. The knuckle-boom hoists money
Onto trucks. Those who can, run off and scream.

I must decide to live without the trees,
Their other lives and old geographies.
The lake goes here. The gullies will be smoothed
To grassy fields where Charolais stand and dream.
The dam goes here. The road across to fields
Lapped by the perfect lake, stumps left for bass,
For where my neighbors' children have to drown
In August because the day swims in heat
And I haven't any children of my own.

At breakfast all my horses stand and look
One way—from the barn, off into the trees.
The horses accuse me and will not eat.
The noise from the woods is noise from the woods,
Not ghosts, not dying birds, not my self-respect.
These horses will not eat. Not while the trees
Are falling in long screams, while at my feet
The deer collapse whose lives have been corrected
In this, no place to bring a lover to.

The Monday Before Thanksgiving

The swamped sun setting behind the water oaks
Shoots fire across my pasture and my pond,
Past barn and house, and across the road
Into the burnished butterfly pines. Narrow your lids
And your last hopes. All these Alabama trees
Light up like Maine. *Alabama: State of Mind.*
What's wrong is the tragedy of light, the fire
Shot flat through trees in that last flash
We see before the great mad bombs must take us out.
The sun hisses and slips like shit into the swamp.
This morning I promised myself I'd transplant
The roses some fool planted where the cows cross
Coming home. For two years I've waited for his irony
To drop in on me like light from a far off star.
What returns is the realtor carried back by her own
Prismatic sonic booms: dwarf yellow, giant red,
And these, the golden white they call moon sun.
What a card! And I without the courage to see them
For what they are, the names of trash. I prune them
Down to stumps. I dig in. I uproot. I do my best
To spare the fine hairs of the roots, the dark webs
More felt than seen in the small light I have left.
Around me the livestock clamor to be fed. The dogs
Chase pullets up and down the lot. One horse will not
Stop striking his shod forefoot against the metal gate,
The clang insistent as a bell. A pair of turkey hens,
Two bronze phoenixes done up in sunset kerosene,
Roost like vultures on the rattling metal gate.
Christmas and Thanksgiving are their cooking names,
Talismans against the cowardice I cannot face.
The horse will not stop striking time against the gate.
From the weedy dam the ducks and geese peer down

And the dogs chase one doomed hen across the pasture,
Through barbed wire and off into the swamp.
Their cries grow faint and the sun goes out like that,
Like danger fading, the air going cooler and cooler.
The roots of the roses do not easily let go; the thorns
Hold back from the night the last of the day's heat.
You dig like that—with ungloved fingers deep
Into the dirt until what you feel is quiet and dark,
Until what you feel is finally cold.

Researching Lost Time

I say we will have no more marriages. Those
that are married already—all but one—shall
live: the rest shall keep as they are.
                                    —Hamlet

1. *Legions of the Confederate Dead*

The lost parameters of an old war press in.
His chest heaves and in his eyes his blood isn't his;
It's the sorrow of doomed animals who will be saved.
Now's the time for all of us to run away.
The thought struggles in a rubbery skull, the changing
Boundaries of the war itself keep me from catching it.

Outside my window five trees, pecans, hover
Bald and breaking over old shells, a muddy lawn
And a legion of the Confederate dead. More ever than died
Here, in Tuscaloosa.
I mention them because, between war and wounds
And the perpetual gripes of dying, they press
Their handsome faces against my screens and mutter things.
They breathe discontent: *We know* you *won't forget us*
Left out here in the cold rain falling to avoid
the Yankee shells. You wouldn't dare forget us.

Think: these days just happen. You sit back. You mix
Memory and discovery and, instead of love or dreams,
The evening that might arrive in dreams, you find you own
A backyard full of dead men who were once as young as you,
And younger, and lovers, and presumably happy.
Now, with their faces pressed against your screens,
You think: it rains harder; the rain will wash them out.
But it won't. It can't. It wasn't meant to.

So you sit. Sit with your face pressed against theirs,
Pressed like cheese through cloth until features
Sliver into crumbs. Come. We're meant to sit so close
To this we can't miss any of it. Let's say: None
Of these Confederate dead are here pushing against
The inside like Halloween kids will push doorbells
Just to say: Hi! Life or Death? Slick choices.

The kids are there, the wet babies, their wounds red
And sentimental, their lips like dead leaves
Wind-blown and rain-stuck to the screens.
Offer them candy, education, a dry bed here
On the other side. Their faces are the Baptist's look
At heaven. Gethsemane, the garden, is awash in faces
Begging all the questions. Nothing can deny these men
Dying more than a hundred years, as imperative
As scenery, more to be trusted. Their eyes insist:
Here we are, Tom, better than the trees, the dogtrot,
The tractor shed, the trampled fences, better
Than you; the spite which shouldn't matter now.

And I say silly things like: You are the forced dreams
Of a drunk's imagination. And they say that's precise.
They've frightened the dogs and they're stopping up
The exits. The dollar falls and the white race worries
For its genes and gasoline goes extinct and they still
Run their faces, lovely as they are, into my eyes.
So these are their parameters tonight.
When they laugh they hold hands to their faces to keep
The flesh from falling off. Because it's not time yet.
At which point I must ask: Who of you has never waved
A white flag at this insistence? Everyone gives up.

2. *Dancing and the Martial Arts*

It's either too late or too early. The dance is over
And the lights are turned down and only I notice.
When dawn reaches the Black Warrior River the water
Runs red, the thick mud saved by its own baptism.
From the Commandant's portico we can't see the river.
All we can do is imagine. Behind us, someone asks
That the orchestra play again. The waltz is empty, but not
Because no one dances. We're on the portico to watch the sun.
A cab turns from the boulevard onto the mansion drive.
Along the boulevard the town will someday plant oaks,
Let them grow; the plan is to mount plaques on them, one
For each dead soldier. The trees do age and grow
And the bronze names grow in and grow valuable. Then,
In another war, we pry out the plaques and sell them
For shell casings and we profit. The trees don't mind.
Someday, no one, not even the trees, will remember
Chancellorsville, and not even the pyrrhic Greeks will own
A better name for Stonewall Jackson's death. Nor will Jackson.
He lies, breathing mud, gunpowder and his own stench.
He remembers the ladies' last party. His bones are soft.
After all, he's one of us and we're not, dead grooms
And greying brides aside, we're not ordinary sentimentalists.

At the annual academy party swords and crutches condition
The art, like gowns and flowers and the dark restless breath
Of Chopin hustling across the floor. The young move slowly
Through the colors. The Commandant's house is done
In late azaleas, the rusting bouquets banked like funerals
Against the walls. Almost from its beginning the war wants us
To come to grips with its end. We dance too slowly;
We're dazed by it all. The receiving line grows longer,

51

The Commandant's wife older, more willing to cope.
Maybe the war has that effect on us. Maybe we thrive.
Who knows? Maybe the romance takes us in as good as truth.
The night is too warm for dancing, but the music pulls us,
Collides us stepping over the dropped corsages, moving slowly
Among one another, never touching more than we must.
Between waltzes and quadrilles we imagine plans:
Union, dissolution, reunion.
Because parting makes sweet sorrow and breeds sons.

We can see the time when the last young man will leave
To fight. He shouldn't go. He wasn't meant to. We can see
The academy going under, the flames up. We can see
Our hostess, historic, as she stomps out fires and runs
To save the house. And it's sad how her comedy scares off
History as well as love.

The last to go with his batsman and his sword is thin,
Weak and unbetrothed. He leaves his mother crying.
On the battlefield he writes pointed love sonnets in blood.
He is always remembered: *Our best, our sweetest soldier.*
He succeeds. The school is going under. In the dirt.
We had to plant our faces and our futures in the red clay
No one should have to own. If we hadn't, we would've.
The knowledge still consoles us, like sunlight on the porch.

3. *The Prisoner of War*

If I had known you when my son died I would've thought
Of you. Time played mean tricks on us. The moonlight.
That day we went so slowly under. My wife and I.
We were like lice crawling each other for room to hide.
The left-overs are quiet: a bathtub, a carpet, the carcasses

Of two dogs, some cats and a few birds snared for their food.
Outside, the pines boiled grey like old soldiers
And in the parlor a beautiful tall clock was chewing
The best parts of our lives. Her grandmother's commode
Fell three storeys into the cellar. Nothing's been stored.
There's nothing left to eat. A knock at the door
And outside there were geese flying over.

My wife and I and you were playing cards in the study.
She was winning and we were talking about the weather
And the geese and if ever we could figure out direction.
Then we'd know what to expect.
When the knock came again we understood:
We'd been talking about the door, about its being locked.
We expected the knock would come and so you said:
If the winds are right and their flight even
They must be going north. Look for moss
On certain sides of the trees in the garden.

We needed your lore to fool us. We went out
To the garden, pressed into the trees, and watched.
The geese flew home. And you may have been right.
The trouble is, there was then no way of knowing.
There were only the geese, out of gunshot, flying
Crazily on, and us, hungry in the garden, thinking
It mattered. We would have eaten even the crows.
For that, we'd have eaten people. My son, for instance,
Who lingers like a name I'm afraid to speak on my lips
And in her gut where you can hear him growl.

The moon goes on. Sooner or later.
The geese fly past and we go back to our cards

In the study. Left alone, the clock dies. The door.
When things solve themselves, they die.
When we speak of the weather, it's not cold or clouds
Or directions, not the pecans or the texture
Of thin squirrels that concern us.
The last news was that folks had taken hold somewhere,
Up north perhaps, and the message is: *We'd sooner die*
On account they took the cows, they said their generals
Was shot. Send food. A pink flame, like a Negro's tongue,
Is eating down the house. Are you still here?
In the face of all this we must stay casual.

There's no knock at the door. No weather.
The geese, when they fly, fly into another story.
This has nothing to do with you.
You were never a prisoner of war in my house
When my wife fed you and I entertained you with cards
And books, when we were never closer than brothers,
When the knock we expected was your death and we fasted
To avoid it. It was never that. Nor was it my wife,
Crazy, drunk, loving us, and her out in the garden
Chasing the spectres away. You aren't here.
I tell the enemy soldiers: We couldn't let him join
This feast; he watched to death from the barn.
The soldiers leave. Our victory builds itself out of
These calamities. You die trapped in the barn.
And this is the easiest part, the way you die.
My wife and I are playing cards in the study.
The soldiers stop in front of the house and call out:
All our generals have died in the war! Feed us!
Out, over the fields, we see the geese flying slowly away
And we wonder where or why. Then the knock.

One after another the realities fall off like blind scales.
Unimportant lives never lived, things that don't matter.

You come in from the kitchen. You admit everything.
The unreal soldiers deployed on the lawn are here
To take you away. You have never been here.
You go to the garden to meet them, then you turn
To face us through the study windows. You say many things
Distorted through the wet screens. You make surrender easy.
I look up from all this and see the corpse of my eight-
Year-old son in the hayloft. He thinks there's a war
Going on. He wants to turn you into the enemy. He changes
His mind when they come for you and they must shoot him.
His blood spoils half a ton of hay. It may well have been him
We've heard knocking about these last few days.

Among the Missing

The bay filly tied to the stoutest apple tree
Finds the right height sucker to break and put
Her left eye out. She is crying her left eye out.
Already the ooze of half her world is what I get
For my stupidity. With her face to the sun,
Her muzzle trapped by the small green apples,
She lets the black stud mount. Sour, green maternity.
She broods. This half of what she'll ever see
Right now, through sharp leaves, the sunlight dapples.

Waterskiing Through Middle Age

My boat surging away pulls you out and up.
In the cove behind us your lovely daughter Mary,
Tan, blonde and supple as a perfect lung, shouts.
She's sliding the long waterfall down to the beach.
Who knows what visitations we have missed?
You lift your left foot, drop that ski, balance
Everything. You list. You turn. You spray
White water in an arc that shines and has to last.
Who says the lake is hard? Your best friends
Lie to you about your age. You watch the rope
Quiver, a yellow line through August's long delay.
When you can, you turn back to her and wave.
The trees have blended, the steep shore dropped away.
Careful. Our small dark friends are going fast.

Exit from the Hotel Lexington

The manager has posted warnings
In English, French, German, Japanese:
I will be silent, I will not stay too late,
And should my dripping shower rot
Its way through twenty-seven floors,
I will pay, his notice says, I will
To have this all again rebuilt.
A Lufthansa pilot runs the elevator down.
Among the ferns a Samurai tends bar.
This could be Lisbon, the war not yet begun.
The bell-hop palms his jingling pockets
And once again the skinny Cuban waiter
Offers me, point-blank, his gun.
The back-bar is ebony, trimmed with gilt.

Forty-eighth Street is walking me west
Toward dissolution, pushing me through
October, the cold late Sunday afternoon.
Diamond merchants tote black Homburgs,
Earlocks, black cases full of jewels
Into the evening they hope is safe.
Sewer gases raise the lost heat of summer,
Lift the cold island we all move through.
I must push west, toward Times Square,
Forty-second Street. I still smell trouble,
Small demeaning sins, loss of what is now.
When done I'll return to the hotel.
The Jews by then will have all gone home.
Again, one life will not have been enough.

The Cannibal Murders on Brick Kiln Road
Cape Cod, 1882

We heard yesterday, over the dunes, animals scream.
Or children. We found gulls eating a woman.
We have been told that in the White Mountains drops
Of blood make purple flowers in the soft snow,
Weighting it against the people who live below.
In the western desert snakes eat their way out
Of craters of sand, grow wings and fly in the night.
I myself have seen the sea retreating and fish
Left dreaming in their dry beds. One night
Towers sprang up, lasted a day, then burned.
This morning some men left town with cages to give
To the gulls. Birds and men seem to have disappeared.

Citizens are all up for the warning, all skeptical
Of dry days and ancient enmities. Their eyes go first.
They see wrong colors, blood and snow out of season.
Flesh is falling away in pieces from their bones.
Discouraged, they speak doubly of a new world
And a broken hold, the killer in their midst.
Famine lingers in the last repairs Falmouth made
In the brickwork around the Green. The town clock
Gives up. The statue's dead. The people starving.
So our road makes history. Each crime we carry
To the water is a wife and child. Binding pale flesh,
Anchor chains rattle psalms for the gulls' responses.
Gulls and chains, antiphonies of a journey, flawed notes
Like crumbs seeding the road running out behind us.
The sea breathes at us and the sun burns everything
To the center. I know. I am the man who makes the bricks.
My friends think, because of me, they are saints
In trouble. I watch them return to the sea

Like crabs scuttling sideways over the hot sand,
Chased by Mayflies out of season, by blindness
And the time of day. But life was never easy with us.
Life is best late in the afternoon, the view full
In the near southeast of thunderclouds building
Past Vineyard Sound, like sanctuary mountains, reached.
Fiddler crabs claw like votaries the ways out
Of wet sand. They leave behind their filling holes
And the flies settling on the kelp, like the past.
The tide washes in, cool with the moon and evening,
To wipe the sun's breath from the closing track.
Nothing is as it should be. Night never comes, really.
A fire spins and multiplies the sand. Blind shells
Ride the boiling sea in one direction, out.

The whole town is heading east and south in a change
Of attitude—toward the beach, dried before each step.
They are retracing the migrations. They are trying.
A tribe of them is going, not really single file, with no
Great distances between them. They find comfort written
Heel to toe, two by two, in the ongoing dust.
I wish I did not have to leave my kiln, not while
The force of day on day is beating my clay
Into the mirrors I want to pass among my friends
Who will be found later, dead of hunger, on the road.

Their teeth fall out. They plant each beside a tree
Along the road. They can hear snakes spring up behind them,
Grow leather wings, as we expected, and hover,
Demanding change, that they be votaries, rekindling
The belief, the promise of dominion over things
Which crawl and bake under the sun. I fire up my kiln.

Mine are the last scrub trees before the ocean,
Pine, oak, getting no reward from the salt I feed the sea.
Look. The ladies list in the wind, take every chance
To shade from burning the bones of their children.
When they run, I will pretend to fall behind,
But I will break into the weapons of their enemy,
To teeth still wedged with meat.

When there were evenings to be surrendered to ideas
These people claimed that all the women from the Bible
Used to come to dance upon our beach. Holy mothers,
High priestesses, the matriarchs who spun a tribe
From sand, a king from cactus. They see I am the last
To arrive, a cannibal, a ghoul, eater of dead children,
Dry clay and graveclothes. And I say that they are now
Dead vines, dead tendrils, dried onto the bricks
Which have fallen away from their various closed gardens.
Among so many I find it hard to be pleasing.
The last food sustains the town, this neck, my neck,
These bones of a gull in his infinite parts.

Losses

Friday afternoon. Have run past the retarded
From the hospital, small Cro-Magnon ladies
Walking their moony faces into town.
It is almost Christmas, almost Halloween.
Dropped combs and broken pencils marked the ground.

Monday evening. The ladies have been blessed.
Their extra arms and legs dropped off like scales.
The path around the quad my miles beat
Has made the dangerous flat planet nearly round.
Present? wanna present? wanna present? want?
One woman said. Her fingers flexed.
Her black eyes swam like fish. My heart was cold.

Thursday night. Mother didn't die today.
The avenue I run stopped short of town
Where the ladies went because it is the thing
They do. Hard rain and mud made going slow.
My feet splayed out at every corner turned.

The Mongol ladies have these songs they sing.
They love me now is what they try to say.

September 1, 1983

In memory of KAL flight 007

Like a rhyme told on toes the pigs in the bed
Of the passing truck are off. *We're off!*
And their eyes aren't really mirrors,
Their snouts snuffling through the bars don't speak.
The beautiful world hasn't failed them once again.
Look! The sunset opens. Bright light falls out
Of the sky. Let's gather up and save the merely dead.
Let's make the headlines fit the neighbor's pigs.

Everyone knows that this is a killer road.
But I can't tell the boy. His dead dog is load
Enough. *Son,* I say, *can I carry you home?*
He looks up until I'm through.
Trouble is, the goldenrod's too high, the poke
Weed berries are just too purple to believe.
His dog is really dead. It's my house, my road,
My beery grief. *Believe me, boy, I grieve.*

Being drunk is easy. I look up from the porch,
Up from my beer. The sky is so doomed, so rare
I want a photograph, so blue I want to swim
Out of my sticky bones. At last, tonight, it's clear
What I expect from my life. Up through the gate the lurch
Of my neighbor's truck. Back from the market
The squeal of the saved pigs. Out of the terrible scream
The smiles. This, this, this is what I have done.

The Saint and Her Betrayer

1.

I am in the chicken yard.
Tenuous hexagonal wires rise around me
Like a veil, irrecoverable, I hold
Away from my face.
Distance does it.
Blood wedding.
The hens play castanets and sympathize.

Once
Two women
In their extraordinary shades of spring green,
Poplar and pine, embraced: arms
And tongues breathing this art
Nobody seems to mind
But the men who must chop themselves down.

2.

The bank calendar's October poem:
  Cares Fall
    Like Autumn Leaves
      With a Savings Plan

We stand at the fire barrel
And plan and warm our hands
Like old men preparing for weather.
Soon it'll be wet ashes and cold.

The bank cracks
The cattle eat cash
The light in the embezzler's eye
Begins to burn out

Let the bank plan
The light cracks, the song cracks,
The painter's sky gives in like plaster

And in the trees behind the hill
A gray sea inflates drop by drop
The Southern winter indulging October.
He is laughing. He is another story.

3.

This is lunacy, the road
Rising and a car drives up.
A boy hides in the storm pit
Behind my house. This is crazy,
What I want him to say,
What he won't say when the car stops
And those in the know tumble out
Like tourists stopped for a meal.

Who is he?
The subject? betrayer?
Another story where all things are equal,
A long novel imported from Russia,
A phase like a month one passes through
Getting places, October when he turns up
For heat and to turn back the clock,
A long novel, a train, both of us,
Arriving on time: from the bank where,
We've been told, our assets have turned
To leaf and safety deposits won't do.

So who is he, trapped
In another story where daddy is a lark
And tragedy funnels itself
Through a hole in the skin?

4.

The amber eye glares up at me.
I close one hand over his head.
I have his attention now, though his eye
Is shut out. I use a serrated knife.
The edges bite through
Feathers and skin, roughly
What holds us together. The head drops,
The eye still flashing
And the body released flashes into the wire.
The cage is alive with this frenzy.

From the hill if he looks what he sees
On the floor of the coop are the heads
Of seven roosters turning the future
Into asters white and large as snow.
Their bodies, strung up by the feet, drain
Down the fenceposts and into the dirt.
They have apostles for wings.
Hens peck at the blood, turn over the heads,
Peck at their droppings, cackle at blood,
Nothing sweet, nothing better.

I gather their heads in a sack. Truly
Nothing is delicate like the light sifting
Into the coop under the pines or hard

Like the kitchen light over the sink
Where I stand shifting from one foot
To the other, tired of work and wet feathers.

5.

I knew a woman like a nickname
Following soldiers into winter camp:
Miranda, Magdalene,
Skeptical to the very end
Or till spring saints them

And the weather cracks.
What I discovered about her was so
Matter-of-fact, so *ordinary* it undid us both.

Looking ahead to December I find
The Bank has given a silhouette of Bethlehem
And the legend we will live by then.

6.

Whenever he wants me I am out in the garden
Tending to marigolds. Or gathering eggs in the coop.
It's November now, the sky a blue too painful
To remark and the light drops like coins
Into a cushion of grass. The marigolds have gone
Stiff and black, unlovely.
I gather the seedheads for spring.
I have sand in my shoes and my clothes in the breeze
Shape me like skin. I pull up the last
Of everything, stalks, vines, and like in particular

The feel of the dirt dropping in clumps
From the roots. It's the secret that kills me.

7.

We are like bloodroot, like hens
Eating dirt, building ourselves
Bit by bit, like bloodroot
Sprouting in dirt,
Like saints
Slipping out of their clothes.

8.

A yellow jacket is battering itself to death
Against a stone. The martin house shakes
On its staff in the wind. The birds seem
To chase their prey into another country.
I will deliver in May. The flies and the birds
Will be back. And the heat like a secret
That kills. He will be back.

The roses, the roosters, need pruning.
The compost begs to be turned
Toward moisture and light.

I am tacking rooster feet to the barn boor
And I have thoughts like other people's songs.

Carnegie Mellon Poetry

1975
The Living and the Dead, Ann Hayes
In the Face of Descent, T. Alan Broughton

1976
The Week the Dirigible Came, Jay Meek
Full of Lust and Good Usage, Stephen Dunn

1977
How I Escaped from the Labyrinth and Other Poems,
    Philip Dacey
The Lady from the Dark Green Hills, Jim Hall
For Luck: Poems 1962-1977, H. L. Van Brunt
By the Wreckmaster's Cottage, Paula Rankin

1978
New & Selected Poems, James Bertolino
The Sun Fetcher, Michael Dennis Browne
A Circus of Needs, Stephen Dunn
The Crowd Inside, Elizabeth Libbey

1979
Paying Back the Sea, Philip Dow
Swimmer in the Rain, Robert Wallace
Far From Home, T. Alan Broughton
The Room Where Summer Ends, Peter Cooley
No Ordinary World, Mekeel McBride

1980
And the Man Who Was Traveling Never Got Home,
    H. L. Van Brunt
Drawing on the Walls, Jay Meek
The Yellow House on the Corner, Rita Dove
The 8-Step Grapevine, Dara Wier
The Mating Reflex, Jim Hall

1981
A Little Faith, John Skoyles
Augers, Paula Rankin
Walking Home from the Icehouse, Vern Rutsala
Work and Love, Stephen Dunn
The Rote Walker, Mark Jarman
Morocco Journal, Richard Harteis
Songs of a Returning Soul, Elizabeth Libbey

1982
The Granary, Kim R. Stafford
Calling the Dead, C. G. Hanzlicek
Dreams Before Sleep, T. Alan Broughton
Sorting It Out, Anne S. Perlman
Love Is Not a Consolation; It Is a Light, Primus St. John

1983
The Going Under of the Evening Land, Mekeel McBride
Museum, Rita Dove
Air and Salt, Eve Shelnutt
Nightseasons, Peter Cooley

1984
Falling From Stardom, Jonathan Holden
Miracle Mile, Ed Ochester
Girlfriends and Wives, Robert Wallace
Earthly Purposes, Jay Meek
Not Dancing, Stephen Dunn
The Man in the Middle, Gregory Djanikian
A Heart Out of This World, David James
All You Have in Common, Dara Wier

1985
Smoke From the Fires, Michael Dennis Browne
Full of Lust and Good Usage, Stephen Dunn (2nd edition)
Far and Away, Mark Jarman
Anniversary of the Air, Michael Waters
To the House Ghost, Paula Rankin
Midwinter Transport, Anne Bromley

1987
Some Gangster Pain, Gillian Conoley
Other Children, Lawrence Raab
Internal Geography, Richard Harteis
The Van Gogh Notebook, Peter Cooley
A Circus of Needs, Stephen Dunn (2nd edition)
Ruined Cities, Vern Rutsala
Places and Stories, Kim R. Stafford

1988
Preparing to Be Happy, T. Alan Broughton
Red Letter Days, Mekeel McBride
The Abandoned Country, Thomas Rabbitt